STEM Projects in MINECRAFT™

The Unofficial Guide to
Science Experiments in
MINECRAFT™

RYAN NAGELHOUT

PowerKiDS press

New York

Published in 2019 by The Rosen Publishing Group, Inc.
29 East 21st Street, New York, NY 10010

First Edition

Editor: Greg Roza
Book Design: Rachel Rising
Illustrator: Matías Lapegüe

Photo Credits: Cover, pp. 1, 3, 4, 6, 8, 10, 12, 14, 15 ,18, 20, 22, 23, 24 (background) Evgeniy Dzyuba/Shutterstock.com; pp. 4, 6, 8, 10, 12, 14, 16 (insert) Levent Konuk/Shutterstock.com; p. 8 Africa Studio/Shutterstock.com; p. 12 iamlukyeee/Shutterstock.com; p. 13 Dmytro Balkhovitin/Shutterstock.com; p. 14 jannoon028/Shutterstock.com; p. 16 Katvic/Shutterstock.com; p. 17 chinahbzyg/Shutterstock.com;p. 19 Dmitry Kalinovsky/Shutterstock.com; p. 20 Zhao jian kang/Shutterstock.com; p. 22 mirana/Shutterstock.com.

Cataloging-in-Publication Data

Names: Nagelhout, Ryan.
Title: The unofficial guide to science experiments in Minecraft / Ryan Nagelhout.
Description: New York : PowerKids Press, 2019. | Series: STEM projects in Minecraft | Includes glossary and index.
Identifiers: ISBN 9781538342565 (pbk.) | ISBN 9781538342589 (library bound) | ISBN 9781538342572 (6pack)
Subjects: LCSH: Minecraft (Game)–Handbooks, manuals, etc.–Juvenile literature. | Minecraft (Game)–Juvenile literature.
Classification: LCC GV1469.35.M535 N34 2019 | DDC 794.8–dc23

Manufactured in the United States of America

CPSIA Compliance Information: Batch #CWPK19. For Further Information contact Rosen Publishing, New York, New York at 1-800-237-9932

Contents

Mine Science

Minecraft is a game that starts simple. You get dropped into a world with no tools but many **resources** around you. After chopping some wood, you can make tools to mine stone and then start searching in caves. After a lot of digging and fighting off **mobs**, you'll have enough resources to do some really cool things.

Many of the items in *Minecraft* can be found in the real world, and the game follows some of the same rules our world does, too! That means, just like in real life, we can do science in *Minecraft!*

pickaxe

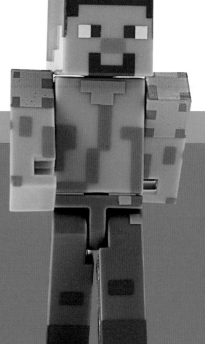

MINECRAFT MANIA

Resources such as gold, iron, and diamonds are all found in real life and in *Minecraft*, while redstone is a special resource found only in the game. You can use all of these things to do experiments, though!

The Crafting Table

Before you make most things in *Minecraft*, you need to build a crafting table. You can make a crafting table out of four wooden **planks**, which you can make from blocks of wood. A crafting table lets you make lots of different things in *Minecraft*, including tools such as shovels, axes, and swords.

If you're playing in Creative **mode**, you'll have any resource available in the game right away. Playing in Survival mode, however, means you have to find the resources you need to craft things. This can take a lot of time and exploring to find the right items for an experiment!

MINECRAFT MANIA

You can mine a crafting table with any tool and pick it up. (An axe works fastest, though.) That way you can move it around as you work on your experiments.

Different *Minecraft* tools are faster at mining or "picking up" certain objects—and some won't mine certain things at all. Experiment a bit with different kinds of axes, shovels, and pickaxes and some wood, dirt, sand, stone, ores, and gravel.

CRAFTING TABLE

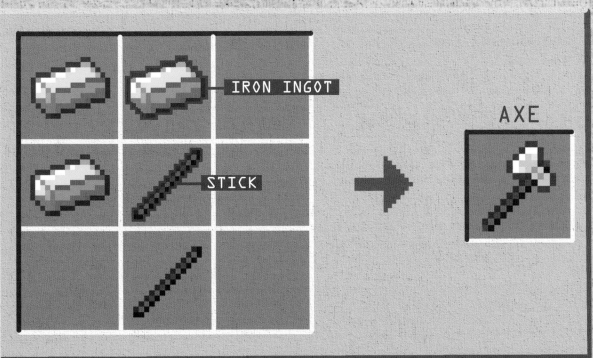

IRON INGOT

STICK

AXE

Blowing Up

If you're playing in Survival mode, you need to watch out for monsters—including creepers. Let one get too close to you and it will blow up—sometimes taking you and whatever you're working on with it! But when you kill a creeper before it can blow up, it might drop something you can use to blow things up, too: gunpowder.

You can use gunpower and sand to make TNT, which creates an explosion you can control. You can place a TNT brick near something and then light it to destroy a lot of blocks at once.

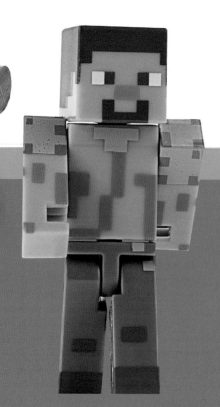

dynamite

MINECRAFT MANIA

You can experiment to see how big an explosion you can create with one block of TNT versus two, three, or even 10 blocks. What arrangement works best to dig deep into the ground?

TNT exists in real life too. The letters are short for trinitrotoluene, an explosive yellow **chemical**. Sand isn't used in real TNT, but a type of sand is used in dynamite, another explosive.

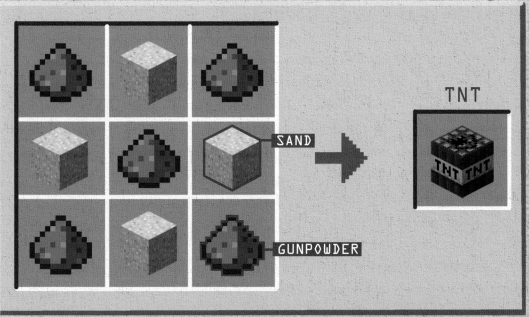

SAND

TNT

GUNPOWDER

Light It Up

You need fire to set off TNT. But just like in real life, it can be dangerous to experiment with fire in *Minecraft*. Make sure to have a few buckets of water nearby—and don't experiment with fire in the real world at all!

However, you can also make fire in *Minecraft* with a flint and steel, which you can use to spark fire on solid blocks. Another way to start fire is with a fire charge, but charges are made with blaze powder. That comes from blaze rods, which are dropped when you kill a monster called a blaze. That can be tricky!

MINECRAFT MANIA

Blaze rods can also be used to make **brewing** stands. These can make **potions** that can give you special powers!

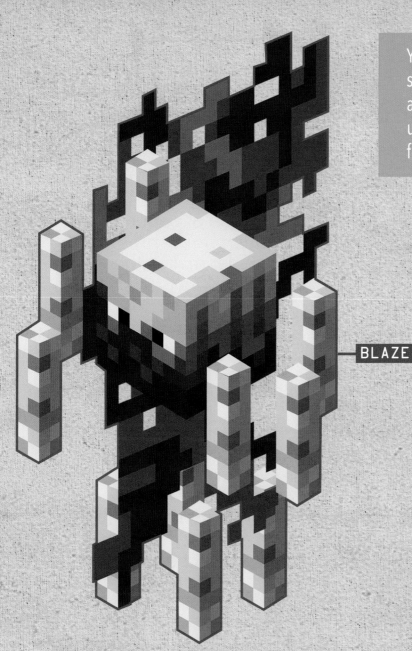

You can make a *Minecraft* flint and steel with one iron ingot and a piece of flint, which is also used to make arrows. You find flint by digging in gravel.

BLAZE

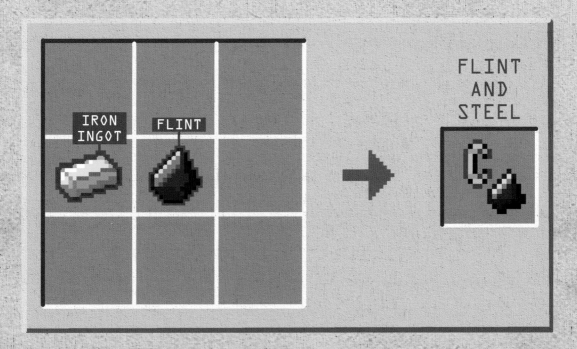

IRON INGOT

FLINT

FLINT AND STEEL

Making Fireworks

You can use gunpowder to make fireworks in *Minecraft*! A single piece of gunpowder and a piece of paper will make a basic firework rocket. More gunpowder makes the rocket stronger. But if you want to have the colorful explosions that real-life fireworks are known for, you have to add a firework star.

Firework stars are made with gunpower, dye (made from plants or other resources), and other items. Add a firework star to a firework rocket recipe to make fireworks that shoot into the air and explode when launched. This is a great way to experiment because there are many cool kinds!

MINECRAFT MANIA

When doing experiments, it's important to keep most of your **variables** the same and change one thing at a time. Then if your results change, you'll know exactly why.

Adding extra ingredients to a firework recipe may make the firework do different things. Try different items and combinations! The recipe shown here makes medium-strength basic blue fireworks.

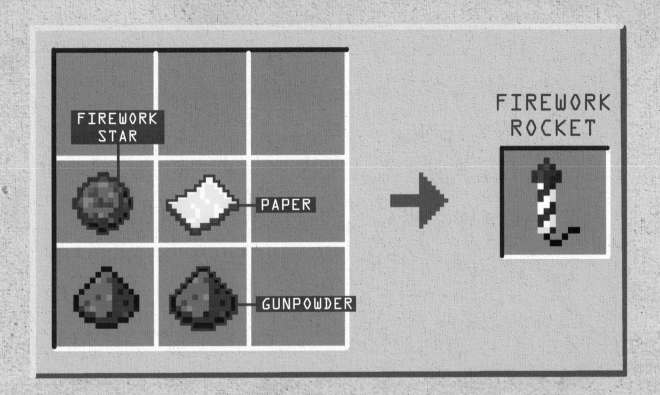

FIREWORK STAR

PAPER

GUNPOWDER

FIREWORK ROCKET

Fun with Redstone

Redstone is a **material** you can use to create circuits or **gadgets**. It comes from redstone ore and it kind of works like electricity! Redstone glows when it's active. You can use buttons, levers, and pressure plates to activate it. You can also put redstone dust down as redstone wire to make the power go farther.

Redstone circuits can make redstone lamps light up. They also activate pistons, which are tools that push something when turned on. Redstone can also be used to make powered rails. When these are activated with redstone, they push minecarts along a track!

MINECRAFT MANIA

Redstone can be used for many experiments. It can power gadgets up to 15 blocks away—but there are ways to extend the signal. Can you experiment and figure them out?

This is a *Minecraft* gadget using redstone dust–a redstone lamp with a lever switch. You can use this simple gaget to light up your *Minecraft* home!

REDSTONE ———

Melting Point

Snow and ice in *Minecraft* act differently than they do in real life. Heat doesn't melt them. You can light a fire right on top of a snow block or an ice block and it still won't melt. However, they *are* melted by light!

You can test how much light is needed to melt ice. Place torches closer to or farther away from ice or snow blocks to see if they melt. You can also try other things that make light, such as **beacons** and furnaces. You can even use redstone to light up torches and lamps to make light. When ice melts, it makes water!

MINECRAFT MANIA

A person can move faster than a minecart when sliding across ice in a two-block-high tunnel. Test it out! Why do you think this happens?

Players, mobs, and items move faster across ice than other surfaces. They slide on it just like we do in the real world! Pour water over ice blocks and see what happens.

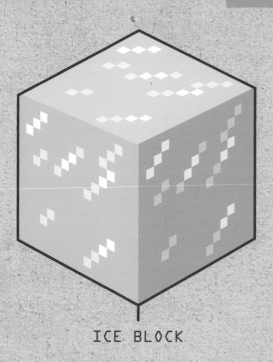

ICE BLOCK

SNOW LAYER ON
A GROUND BLOCK

Using Gravity

Gravity in *Minecraft* is also different than in the real world. Only some bricks will fall if there isn't anything to support them. Dirt, stone, and many other blocks will float if you take away the blocks under them. However, blocks such as sand and gravel will fall until they hit a block that can support them.

You can experiment with gravity with different materials to see if they fall. Be careful, though. A *Minecraft* world may have gravel or sand blocks that are naturally supported by blocks on either side— but if you mess with them, they'll fall out from underneath you or down from over your head!

In the real world, it's not safe to build structures on sand or gravel. These materials can shift and settle under heavy machinery and building supplies.

On Its Own

A hopper is a container with storage space and a funnel-shaped passage. The funnel allows materials stored in the hopper to pass through slowly. You can make *Minecraft* machines that work on their own using hoppers.

The machine at right uses three hoppers to **smelt** ore. The top hopper feeds ore, such as iron ore, into the furnace. The second hopper feeds fuel, such as coal, into the furnace. The furnace smelts the ore and produces iron ingots. The hopper on the bottom catches the ingots and stores them for later use. Once you build this machine and fill the chests with coal and iron ore, it runs all on its own!

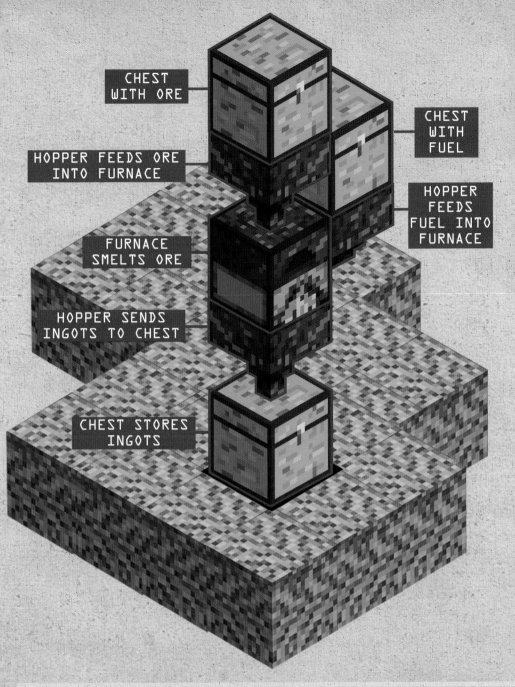

CHEST WITH ORE

CHEST WITH FUEL

HOPPER FEEDS ORE INTO FURNACE

HOPPER FEEDS FUEL INTO FURNACE

FURNACE SMELTS ORE

HOPPER SENDS INGOTS TO CHEST

CHEST STORES INGOTS

In the real world, smelting is a dangerous process that requires high temperatures. We use smelting to produce pure metals, such as iron, gold, and much more.

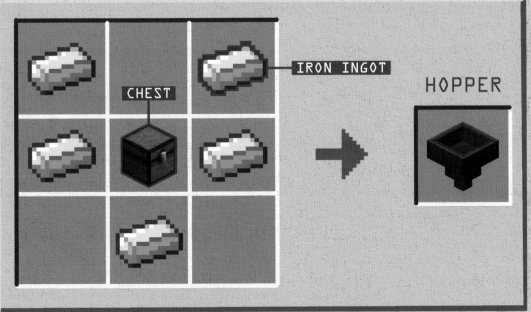

IRON INGOT

CHEST

HOPPER

Making Mods

You can make your *Minecraft* creations even more exciting with modifications, or mods. Using a computer program called ScriptCraft, you can create new blocks, change the way the game functions, and make your own games. Imagine what you could create! You could create new ways to experiment with materials and blocks, or you could set up your very own *Minecraft* science lab.

If you're interested in learning how to create mods in *Minecraft*, visit the website below. You'll find the information needed to get started with ScriptCraft and build your own *Minecraft* mods. **https://scriptcraftjs.org/**

Glossary

beacon: A strong light that can be seen from far away. In *Minecraft*, a beacon is a block that sends a light beam into the sky.

brew: To make a new liquid by mixing things together.

chemical: Matter that can be mixed with other matter to cause changes.

gadget: A small or useful device that is often interesting, unfamiliar, or unusual.

material: Something from which something else can be made.

mob: A moving creature within *Minecraft*. Often used to mean one of the monsters that spawns, or appears, in *Minecraft* at night.

mode: A form of something that is different from other forms of the same thing.

potion: A drink meant to have a special effect on someone.

plank: A heavy, thick board of wood.

resource: Something that can be used.

smelt: Heating ore to separate metals from waste material.

variable: A quantity that may change when other conditions change.

Index

Websites

Due to the changing nature of Internet links, PowerKids Press has developed an online list of websites related to the subject of this book. This site is updated regularly. Please use this link to access the list:
www.powerkidslinks.com/stemmc/experiments